MR. POPS

MR. POPS

By James R. Holland

Barre Publishers, Barre, Massachusetts
1972

Portions of this book first appeared in the
following publications:

Bottom picture on page number 90 was
originally published in Volkswagen's Magazine
Small World.

Pictures on page numbers 14, 18, 25, and 87
(top) appeared in Robin Moore's book *Fiedler:
The Colorful Mr. Pops—The Man and
His Music*. Copyright 1968 by
R. & J. Moore, Inc.

Maestro and author sparking.
(Photo by David Mugar)
James Holland is a film producer for the
Christian Science Center in Boston. A former
contract photographer for *National Geographic Magazine,* Mr. Holland now practices photography for the fun of it. He is
author of one previous book, *The Amazon.*

ACKNOWLEDGMENTS

The creation of this book involved the cooperation of many, many people. The author would like to thank the following for their contributions. Special thanks to John Baehrend, Baldwin Baker Jr., John Cahill, Gordon N. Converse, Sharon Cooper, William Cosel, Nancy Dawson, Helen Devine, Jonathan Fisher, Bert Forbes, Thomas Morris, David Mugar, Thomas D. Perry Jr., Edward Pieratt, Margaret and Gordon Ramsay, Robert Shipman, Bill Shisler, Steve Solomon, Emilie Stuart, Syrl Silberman, Joan and Robert Thompson, George Ward, and Alan Young.

Taking these photographs would have been impossible without the consent and generous assistance of the players of the Boston POPS Orchestra and the staff and management of the Boston Symphony Orchestra. A note of appreciation should also be extended to everyone at Barre Publishers, and the Christian Science Center who provided encouragement and support for this project.

PREFACE

This photographic essay is not impartial. It was written and photographed by one of Arthur Fiedler's most devoted fans. While he went about his business, I took pictures just as they happened. It was my desire to provide a candid view of the Maestro's remarkable personality.

James Holland

This book is dedicated to Ellen, Johanna, Deborah, and Peter.

Fisheye view of Arthur Fiedler conducting an Esplanade Concert.

INTRODUCTION

Arthur Fiedler was born in Boston on December 17, 1894. He was heir to a rich musical heritage which included his father, Emanuel, two uncles—Bernard and Gustav, and a first cousin, Josef Zimbler, all members of the Boston Symphony Orchestra. His mother, Johanna, was an accomplished amateur pianist. His Austrian grandfather and great-grandfather were musicians in the early days of the nineteenth century. "Fiedler" means "fiddler" in old German.

In 1910, Arthur's father retired from the Boston Symphony Orchestra (BSO) and moved his family first to Vienna, Austria, and then on to Berlin, Germany.

During 1911, at the age of sixteen, Arthur decided to pursue music as his career. He was accepted as a student in the exclusive Royal Academy of Music in Berlin. To his own surprise, Arthur discovered that he actually enjoyed his studies, although he was "never too keen about the long hours of practice." In addition to studying the violin, the young Fiedler delved into music history, music theory, and conducting. He also found the time to play in the Berlin String Quartet, a group organized and led by his father, Emanuel. Playing his violin in cafes, teaching music, and playing in theater-pit orchestras provided Arthur with additional money to pay for his tuition.

World War I broke out, but Arthur remained in Berlin studying at the Academy until the spring of 1915 when America was forced into the war. With the aid of friends, Arthur fled Germany to Amsterdam, Holland. Frustrated by the unavailability of jobs, Arthur decided to return to the United States.

Reaching Boston in midsummer, Arthur was given a temporary job in his Uncle Bernard's orchestra at a resort hotel on Nantucket Island. In the autumn, "Uncle Benny" went back to work in the BSO and Arthur accepted a job

Arthur's music spans the generation gap.

Arthur's mother Johanna and his eldest sister Fredericka in 1892.

as violinist in a trio at a hotel in Springfield, Massachusetts.

After three weeks of working in Springfield, Arthur received a phone call from Charles Ellis, Manager of the BSO. Because of his experience, talent, and recommendations, Arthur was accepted without audition as second violinist in the Boston Symphony Orchestra. He was barely twenty years old at the time.

World War I ended and Arthur spent the next several years acquiring a reputation as a playboy. While the young Fiedler was gaining prominence as one of the most fun-loving and eligible young bachelors in Boston Society, the Boston Symphony Orchestra was also undergoing a metamorphosis. Dr. Karl Muck was succeeded by Henri Rabaud, then Pierre Moneux, and in 1924, Sergey Alexandrovitch Koussevitzky, whose arrival coincided with the beginning of Arthur Fiedler's rise to fame.

Since conducting his first professional orchestra as a third year student at the Berlin Academy, Arthur had dreamed of becoming a symphony conductor. In 1925, he began turning these dreams into fact by organizing a group he dubbed the Boston Sinfonietta. His group, comprised of twenty-two musicians (all members of the BSO) became popular all over New England—and neighboring states. Arthur's success with the Sinfonietta led to his selection as conductor of the final 1926 POPS concert, when the regular leader suddenly quit in a rage.

Speculation arose that the young Fiedler might be named to replace Maestro Agide Jacchia, but the BSO management thought differently and they selected Alfredo Casella as director. Arthur was disappointed, but the experience served to make him work harder to achieve his conducting dream. While continuing to play the viola, celesta, piano, organ, and various percussion instruments in the BSO, Arthur was developing another idea. He devoted all his attention to creating a series of free, outdoor, symphony concerts. He overcame every possible kind of obstacle, and on the 4th of July, 1929, Arthur stepped onto the podium of a hastily constructed wooden concert shell and led his orchestra in a booming rendition of Sousa's "Stars and Stripes Forever."

Five thousand curious people gathered on the Esplanade to hear what was advertised as a concert of "symphonic music and popular tunes played by symphony musicians." Even the corps of policemen on hand in case of trouble had little to do but enjoy the music. By the end of the first week in August, more than 200,000 people had attended the free concerts.

In February of 1930, Arthur Fiedler officially became the first Boston-born conductor of the 45-year-old Boston POPS Orchestra. Arthur had definite ideas as to how a popular orchestra should sound. Under previous conductors the popularity of the POPS had waned, but Arthur recognized the problem lay in the selection of music and not in the concept of the series. Since the POPS orchestra is really the Boston Symphony Orchestra "in its spring garb," Arthur knew he was working with many of the world's best musicians. He quickly applied his own experience to creating new programs which mixed just the right amounts of classical, semi-classical, and popular music. Previous conductors had attempted to make the POPS concerts a mere extension of the symphony season. Certain this trend was wrong, Arthur was determined to prove his theory. His first official concert as POPS conductor included Elgar's "Pomp and Circumstance," Verdi's "Fantasia Aida," Ravel's "Bolero," and Herbert's "American Fantasy."

Even in the early days of his career, Arthur was attuned to what his audiences wanted. For Arthur (to quote the famous composer Rossini), "Every kind of music is good, except the boring kind." In his quest for new sounds, the Maestro was one of the first white men to venture into what was then a "black jazz world." He was one of the first to ap-

Emanuel Fiedler, Arthur's father, in 1894.

Photograph taken at Arthur's tenth birthday party in 1904. The Maestro remembers having slyly hidden a new rubber ball in his jacket pocket.

Emanuel Fiedler and young Arthur on holiday at a sea resort on the Baltic Sea in 1922.

The Berliner Streich-Quartet in which both Emanuel (left) and Arthur (right) played during the years Arthur was attending Berlin's Royal Academy of Music.

preciate and orchestrate the haunting melodies of the "Beatles." Good music cannot elude the Maestro for very long. His sense of timing is uncanny. Although he complains of today's "music pollution" (his term for being continually bombarded with music whether it be in the elevator or the dentist's chair), Arthur has always been able to separate the good music from the bad.

In 1941, at the age of 46, Arthur Fiedler proposed to 26-year-old Ellen Mary Bottomley. He had been seeing Ellen for about eight years. Their romance had been a favorite subject of discussion, but the age gap and different religious backgrounds precluded serious speculation of an impending marriage. Their engagement was one of the highlights of the social season, as was their marriage in January of 1942.

World War II brought new duties to the newly married Arthur Fiedler. He and his orchestra played hundreds of USO concerts throughout New England. The POPS also recorded a number of "V-Discs" for use on the Armed Forces Radio Network. But this musical contribution to the overall war effort was not enough for the Maestro. Arthur wanted to help the war effort in a more direct way. So, in 1943, at the age of 48, the POPS leader became an "apprentice seaman" in the United States Coast Guard Temporary Reserve. While on active duty, checking cargoes entering and leaving Boston Harbor, Arthur met an Irishman, John Cahill, who was to become his best friend. Together they turned their small converted cabin cruiser into a gourmet's delight. John and Arthur became two of the best fed sailors in the Coast Guard. It was considered an honor to join them for mess.

"Uncle John" Cahill witnessed the christening of Arthur's two daughters, Johanna and Deborah, and his son, Peter. He has accompanied Arthur on many of the Maestro's cross-country tours, and he shares Arthur's interest in fire chasing or "sparking," as such activity is nicknamed.

Arthur is intensely proud of his two daughters and his son.

In 1971, young Peter Fiedler and his "Rubber Dog Review" rock band made their debut at Symphony Hall. He and Johanna, who had also been a guest narrator, marked the third generation of Fiedlers to play at the POPS. Few things could please Arthur Fiedler more, except maybe to see the fourth generation's debut in the Hall.

Draftee Fiedler and friend at Camp Devens in 1918.

The Maestro guest conducting the orchestra at the North End's Annual "Feast of the Assumption." (Photo by David Mugar.)

Pianist Chuchú Sanromá and Arthur Fiedler taking a stroll around Jamaica Pond in the late 1920's.

Serge Koussevitzky and Arthur conferring shortly before a concert of the Boston Symphony Orchestra. (Photo by Harold Orne)

Young Fiedler looking out the window of painter Mrs. Karl Barth's studio.

Ellen Bottomley in 1943.

The Fiedler family playing with Peter's miniature fire engine.

Johanna and her father arriving at the Esplanade shell in July 1948.

A rare picture of young Arthur Fiedler rehearsing while seated.

While Father looks on, Johanna and Deborah play a piano serenade for their two favorite dolls.

Pablo Casals and Arthur take time for a chat during Arthur's brief visit to Puerto Rico in 1966. (Photo by N. Stoute)

In 1936, seventy-seven-year-old Emanuel Fiedler illustrates how he played at the very first POPS concert. Arthur had just begun his sixth season as POPS leader.

Arthur and Pierre Monteux tuning up prior to a special concert for Monteux's 80th birthday.

An avid boxing fan, Arthur Fiedler playfully sparred with Rocky Marciano in 1955.

(Opposite) During a 1965 visit to Japan, Mr. and Mrs. Fiedler were treated to a round of ceremonies usually reserved for visiting heads of state. Arthur did manage to find time to conduct a fire department band and meet a champion Sumo wrestler.

The Fiedler girls greeting their dad after one of his tours.

Arthur takes time out from work to autograph records in Jordan Marsh's Boston department store.

Arthur arriving at Symphony Hall in his black Volkswagen with the "POPS" license plates.

Arthur's 75th birthday party was celebrated with a special symphony concert. There were speeches, letters of congratulations, lots of gifts including a full-sized fire truck, but the most personal gift was from the orchesta itself. They announced that they would soon present him with a dalmatian puppy.

The presentation took place in Arthur's office. An animal lover, he was delighted with the small dog and he promptly named him "Sparkie II," after his former dalmatian firechasing companion.

Outside his Brookline home with Sparkie II.

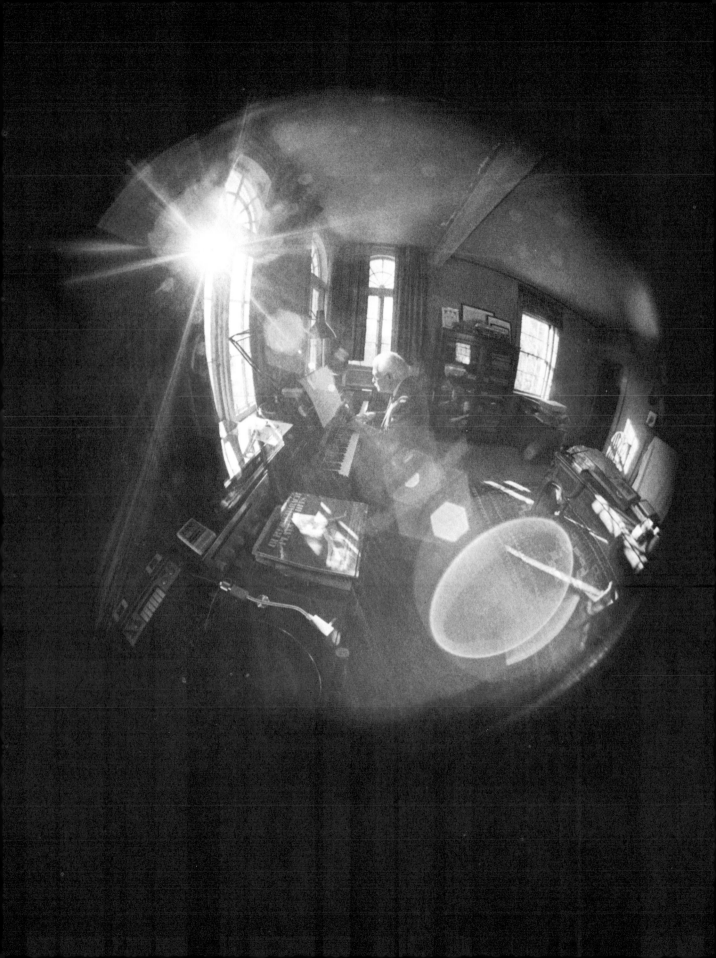

One section of the Fiedler house is separated from the rest by a thick soundproof door. Arthur is a light sleeper. Once awake, he often will sit in bed reading, marking scores, answering correspondence, or listening to music on a stereo or tape recorder. Able to thrive on only a few hours of sleep, Arthur often puts in a full day's work before most people have had breakfast.

Flying is one of the few times that the Maestro is able to rest. If he is not tired, Arthur will open up his briefcase, pull out the conductor's scores for his next concert, and carefully review each detail.

A long-time friend of the New England Conservatory of Music, Arthur joined its president, Gunther Schuller, to co-conduct the Conservatory chorus and orchestra in a special fund-raising effort. (See following pages.)

Washington, D.C. is one of Arthur's regular stops. His eldest daughter Johanna (Yummy, as she is called by her family) lives in the capitol city and she usually meets him at the plane and drives him to his hotel. In the morning, Johanna often arrives at the hotel early enough to join Arthur for breakfast at a small White Tower restaurant across the street.

After Arthur's Kennedy Center rehearsals,
he and Yummy take time for a drink and
conversation.   *Conducting at Kennedy Center.*

Michael Tilson Thomas, Associate Conductor
of the BSO, and Arthur exchange bouquets
of flowers.

On Sunday, March 14, 1971, Arthur began a
cross-country tour with the National
Symphony. In addition to rehearsals and
opening night concert at New York's Lincoln
Center, Arthur used the spare day in
New York to meet with the program staff
to complete planning for the upcoming
television series "Evening at POPS."

*Mrs. Fiedler and Peter Fiedler enjoying
the festivities.*

*Arthur's schedule is so jam-packed, that he
cannot afford to waste either time or words.
Each second is lived to the maximum.
Whatever he is doing, or to whomever he is
talking, that is the most important thing or
person in the world. His complete absorbtion
in the person to whom he is speaking is one
of the secrets of the Maestro's charm.
He makes everyone feel important!*

In early April, 1971, the Boston POPS made its first international tour in ten years. The orchestra departed Logan Airport for London aboard two special Pan American Clippers— one of which was nicknamed "Clipper Boston POPS." This was the first time the entire Boston POPS Orchestra had performed outside the United States.

*London's Royal Albert Hall was the first
stop on the tour. Playing to an enthusiastic
full house, the POPS style of music was
loved by London's live audiences. When the
"St. Louis Blues" march began, so did the
rhythmic clapping and foot stomping.
Louis Synder, music critic for* The Christian
Science MONITOR, *who was traveling with
the orchestra, wrote, "It is doubtful if in
its 100 year history the Albert Hall has
had happier or more vociferous audience
response."*

The second international appearance of the Boston POPS was at a concert in Beethoven Hall, in Bonn, Germany. Guest soloist was Mrs. Joan Kennedy narrating Prokofiev's "Peter and the Wolf."

Although billed as one of the most expensive concerts in postwar Germany, the performances had been sold out months in advance. Senator Edward M. Kennedy was in the audience to witness his wife's performance. (Photos by Edward Fitzgerald)

Following pages: During the POPS season, the austere face of Symphony Hall is relaxed a bit. The seats on the main floor are removed and small round tables with foldup chairs are substituted. A canopy over the stage adds to the festive POPS atmosphere.

Bill Shisler distributes music just prior to concert time.

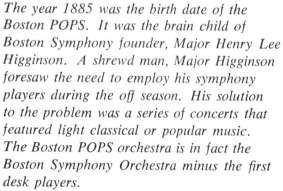

The year 1885 was the birth date of the Boston POPS. It was the brain child of Boston Symphony founder, Major Henry Lee Higginson. A shrewd man, Major Higginson foresaw the need to employ his symphony players during the off season. His solution to the problem was a series of concerts that featured light classical or popular music. The Boston POPS orchestra is in fact the Boston Symphony Orchestra minus the first desk players.

Backstage between numbers.

During intermission, and during portions of the concerts, a small army of waitresses work to serve the audience sandwiches and drinks. For those too young to drink champagne, there is the traditional POPS punch.

Following pages: Arthur and vocalist
Leontyne Price. (Photo by William Shisler)

*William Buckley, Jr. narrated Ogden Nash's
verses at Symphony Hall.*

The Green Room backstage at Symphony Hall is slightly different during POPS season. At the close of the regular Symphony Season, stage hands move in Arthur's portable draft beer dispenser. The Green Room is where Arthur's friends and guests gather. Often, Arthur will personally serve them beer from the tap. He enjoys demonstrating the perfect technique for drawing good draft beer. Here he toasts William Buckley.

Julia Child, better known as "The French Chef" made her Boston POPS debut with Arthur Fiedler early in the season. After narrating "Tubby the Tuba," she took a moment to concoct a special drink for the POPS conductor. Bill Shisler and "Evening at POPS" television producer Bill Cosel observe the happening.

Right: Dave Brubeck, Paul Desmond, and Gerry Mulligan.

DANNY KAYE
AND ARTHUR
FIEDLER
conduct the
BOSTON POPS
PENSION FUND CONCERT
SUNDAY, MAY 16
8:30 P.M.

*Mr. Fiedler conducts:
WASHINGTON POST MARCH
BOLERO
SELECTIONS FROM 'HAIR'

*Mr. Kaye conducts:

The Management simply cannot be responsible for

Danny Kaye came to Boston to conduct the
musicians' pension fund concert and Arthur
was at the airport to meet him. The Maestro
and Danny greeted each other, as fellow
traveler and assistant POPS conductor Harry
Ellis Dickson watched. Danny was still
suffering from a painful accident that had
occurred some months before so he and Arthur
walked arm in arm.

Arthur stops to provide an autograph, and Danny greets Yummy.

*At concert time the next night Arthur
conducted the first segment of the program
and then joined his daughter "Yummy" at a
table in the audience. Mr. Kaye's performance
seemed to delight Maestro Fiedler who found
himself in the unusual role of POPS spectator.*

Arthur at work in the Symphony Hall Music Library. On the desk are two of his recently acquired German fire chief helmets. Anyone who works with the Maestro soon discovers that he is meticulous. This trait is evident in his dress, in his business dealings, and in his music. The thought of conducting a concert without adequate rehearsal makes Arthur boil. He schedules as many practice sessions as possible, and he often keeps the musicians together until their performance is perfect.

The Maestro's extra set of arms belong to Joseph Spotts, Arthur's valet for more than twenty years.

Sesame Street came to the POPS and with it came troops of pre-schoolers. At one point in the program, Arthur turned over his baton to Big Bird for his conducting debut.
Mr. Fiedler added his own percussion whistle to the chorus of "rubber duckies."

Tired and ready to leave for home, Arthur pauses to give last minute instructions about the next morning's recording session.

Top: John Hartford and his Blue Grass Group was only one of the varied "Evening at POPS" television shows.

One of the more interesting highlights of the 1971 Season occurred on May 24th, when Peter Fiedler and his "Rubber Dog Review" Rock Band debuted with the POPS. (Photo by Helen Devine)

*Dizzy Gillespie and his trumpet joined
Arthur at both Boston and San Francisco
POPS concerts. Arthur conducts the San
Francisco POPS for three weeks each summer.*

During a performance of Tchaikovsky's
"1812 Overture," the audience was amazed
to hear the blast of real cannons in the
background. As the cannon fire drowned out
the church bells, smoke poured onto the
stage from the right. Mr. Fiedler smiled,
brought the piece to its conclusion, bowed
to a roar of applause and then made his way
off stage, parting the billowing white clouds
of smoke with his arms as he exited.

Backstage, one of the temporary cannoneers
suggested that the Maestro go back on stage
wearing a fire helmet and carrying a fire axe.
Arthur made note of the idea and saluted his
three man "firing squad," their commander
(who follows the score and signals them
when to fire), and the garbage can that
converts the shotguns' blasts into the
roar of cannons.

The concert is over.

During the actual recording session, Arthur stands atop his podium dressed in his favorite black shirt. A telephone on the podium connects him with the Deutsche Grammaphon engineers in the basement. After completing about an hour of recording, the orchestra takes a break and Arthur goes downstairs to listen to the playback.

On the eve of a recording session, immediately after the regular POPS concert ends, the Symphony Hall stage crew removes the tables and chairs from the auditorium's main floor. A huge curtain is draped across one end of the auditorium's main floor to absorb unwanted reverberation. Partitions separate the various percussion players. Microphones bristle from strategically located stands or hang down from the ceiling.

(Photo by RCA Victor)

In a soundproof room, seated in front of huge speakers, Arthur and Polydor record producer Tom Mowrey listen to the morning's recordings. Every sound is followed on the score and notes are made concerning changes in mixing.

In the early days of wax recordings, the orchestra would have to journey to RCA Victor's sound stage in Camden, N.J. They would also have to play the entire piece perfectly or redo it. POPS' recordings are now available from both RCA Victor and Polydor.

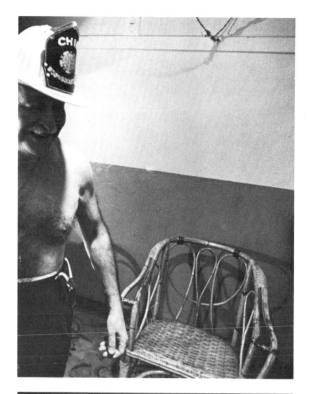

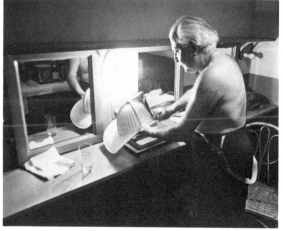

During a concert in Woonsocket, Rhode Island, Arthur was made an honorary fire chief in the city's fire department. After the concert, guests waiting outside his dressing room were amazed to see the Maestro walk past the half-closed door minus his shirt but wearing his new fire helmet. The famous fire buff was dressing to go for a ride on one of the Woonsocket fire trucks.

The excitement of chasing fire trucks of watching the ballet of skilled firemen risking their lives to save others . . . these things help Arthur to unwind—to relax to the point that he can get a good night's sleep. No matter how tired Mr. Fiedler may feel before a concert, by its conclusion he is completely exhilarated. There is some magic about the music, the physical exertion, and the applause. It takes three or four hours after a concert before he can even begin to think about sleep. That's the main reason he chases fires. It's something for him to do when the city is asleep or watching the late movie. It's something he doesn't have to think about because it's completely unrelated to music. Unlike the rest of his disciplined schedule, his sparking is spontaneous. It fulfills his need for adventure!

Big fires are rare. Most of sparking consists of just driving around listening to the police calls and seeing "what's doing." A midnight stop at Dunkin' Donuts provides John, Arthur, and David a chance to warm up.

Arthur Fiedler and John Cahill craning their necks to watch a three alarm fire in Roxbury, Massachusetts.

Arthur's group likes dropping in on the Blarney Stone Bar because it is one of the few places in Boston which serves Guinness Stout on draft. The Maestro is frequently recognized and mobbed by admirers such as these girls from South Boston women's bowling team, the "Columbia Anchorettes."

Opposite: Kenmore Square is one of the many regular stops for Arthur and his sparking cronies. Here, he and David Mugar visit the free medical van and chat with volunteer workers from Massachusetts General Hospital.

"Fire chief Fiedler" loves drinking in small bars, mixing with the characters he meets there, and flirting with the girls. His nights out with the boys remind him of his bachelor days and help keep him young. He exchanges jokes, gossip, and friendly insults with his buddies. His handsome, rugged face radiates excitement. He can relax and be his earthy self.

When Arthur talks about an upcoming concert in Worcester, Massachusetts, his eyes sparkle with delight. He is thinking about the after-concert festivities at the El Morocco Restaurant. "Gourmet Fiedler" likes to "help out" Paul Aboody in the restaurant's kitchen. Here, Arthur takes time out from his meal to smile at the spontaneous floor show put on by one of the guests.

Opposite: Going home.

BOSTON POPS ORCHESTRA

Arthur Fiedler   *Conductor*
Harry Ellis Dickson   *Assistant Conductor*

First violins
Max Hobart,
acting concertmaster
Rolland Tapley
Roger Shermont
Max Winder
Harry Dickson
Gottfried Wilfinger
Fredy Ostrovsky
Leo Panasevich
Noah Bielski
Herman Silberman
Stanley Benson
Sheldon Rotenberg
Alfred Schneider
Gerald Gelbloom
Raymond Sird
William Waterhouse
Amnon Levy

Second violins
Clarence Knudson
William Marshall
Michel Sasson
Ronald Knudsen
Leonard Moss
Ayrton Pinto
Laszlo Nagy
Michael Vitale
John Korman
Christopher Kimber
Spencer Larrison
Ikuko Mizuno
Cecylia Arzewski
Marylou Speaker

Violas
Reuben Green
Eugene Lehner
George Humphrey
Jerome Lipson
Robert Karol
Bernard Kadinoff
Vincent Mauricci
Earl Hedberg
Joseph Pietropaolo
Robert Barnes
Hironaka Sugie*

Horns
Charles Yancich
Harry Shapiro
David Ohanian
Thomas Newell
Paul Keaney
Ralph Pottle

Trumpets
Roger Voisin
Gerard Goguen
André Come
Robert Mogilnicki

Trombones
Ronald Barron
Paul Gay
Kauko Kahila

Tuba
Chester Schmitz

Timpani
Arthur Press

Percussion
Charles Smith
Thomas Gauger
Frank Epstein
Frederick Buda

Harp
Ann Hobson

Piano
Leo Litwin

Organ
Berj Zamkochian

Librarians
Victor Alpert
William Shisler

Stage Manager
Alfred Robison

Cellos
Martin Hoherman
Mischa Nieland
Stephen Geber
Robert Ripley
Luis Leguia
Carol Procter
Jerome Patterson
Ronald Feldman
William Stokking
Joel Moerschel

Basses
William Rhein
Joseph Hearne
Bela Wurtzler
Leslie Martin
John Salkowski
John Barwicki
Robert Olson
Lawrence Wolfe

Flutes
James Pappoutsakis
Paul Fried

Piccolo
Lois Schaefer

Oboes
John Holmes
Wayne Rapier

English horn
Laurence Thorstenberg

Clarinets
Pasquale Cardillo
Peter Hadcock, E^b clarinet

Bass clarinet
Felix Viscuglia

Bassoons
Ernest Panenka
Matthew Ruggiero

Contra bassoon
Richard Plaster

William Moyer, *Personnel manager*
* member of the Japan Philharmonic Symphony Orchestra participating in a one season
exchange with Yizhak Schotten.